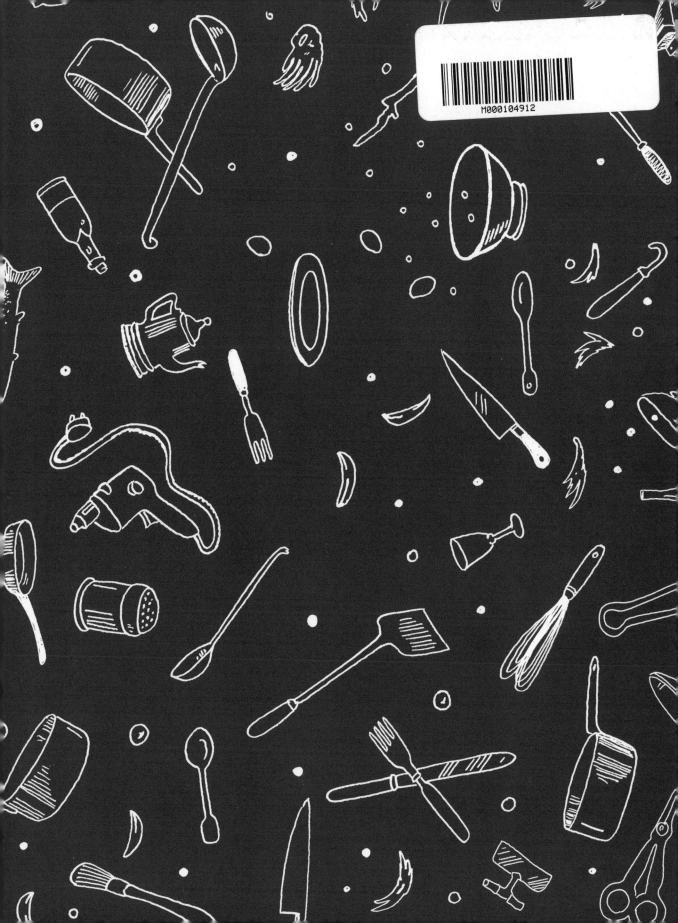

GLEN BAXTER'S

WALMSLEY WAS EXPERIENCING DIFFICULTY WITH THE SEAFOOD SALAD

· Glen Baxter ·

GOURMET GUIDE

BLOOMSBURY

First published 1997

Copyright © 1997 by Glen Baxter
except those drawings as shown copyright © *The New Yorker*
1989, 1991, 1990, 1991, 1990

The moral right of the author has been asserted

Bloomsbury Publishing Plc,
38 Soho Square, London W1V 5DF

A CIP catalogue record for this book is available
from the British Library

ISBN 0 7475 3736 4

10 9 8 7 6 5 4 3 2 1

Printed in Great Britain by Butler and Tanner Ltd, Frome

to ALAN DAVIDSON

定 価

author and driving force behind
Petits Propos Culinaires, whose
boundless enthusiasm and inspired
observations have led directly to
the publication of this volume.
It is upon his imperial snood that
the entire burden of blame must
therefore be placed.

Contents

BASIC INGREDIENTS

PREPARATION

AT TABLE

BASIC INGREDIENTS

Nottingham Picnic Spinach

Ingredients:

1 bicycle with saddlebag
2lbs spinach
1 bottle Lee Kum Kee oyster sauce
1/2oz butter (unsalted)
1 pair pliers
box matches

Cooking Method:

Cycle to designated picnic area. Dismount.
Remove cover from bicycle bell. Light fire.
Hold inverted bell top over flame with
pliers. Toss in butter. Gradually empty all
spinach from saddlebag into bell cover.
Garnish with five drops oyster sauce. Toss
three times and serve immediately.

Himmel und Erde
A delicacy from the Rhine area

Ingredients:

8lbs apples
14lbs potatoes
10 blutwurst sausages
11/2 lbs butter
4oz lard

Cooking Method:

Peel and chop the apples and potatoes.
Boil in water for 18 minutes. Drain.
Pound remains to a purée using a wooden
mallet. Set to one side.
Fry sausages in the lard till cooked.
Toss apple and potato purée into the
sausage pan and amalgamate. Empty into
small oak barrel (preferably one served
with elvish figures brandishing gherkins
and sprigs of rosemary in the Rhenish
style) and bring to the table. (Serves one).

LEAVING JAMES ALONE WITH ROOT VEGETABLES
WAS NOT ALWAYS SUCH A GOOD IDEA

"PERHAPS I COULD RE-AWAKEN YOUR INTEREST
IN LETTUCE" ANNOUNCED THE STRANGER

" JUST WHERE EXACTLY IS THIS SPECIAL
MARINADE OF YOURS THEN, GUNTHER ? "
BLURTED THE TWO VICTIMS

BRENDA TOOK HER HIGHBALLS VERY SERIOUSLY

"THEY HAVE ASSURED ME IT'S A
BAVARIAN DELICACY" NOTED KEN UNEASILY

SOMETIMES, AS A TREAT, WE WERE
ALLOWED TO LOOK AT A GLASS OF
WARM WATER FOR A FEW MINUTES

BALLANTINE CALCULATED THAT HE WAS
APPROACHING THE SAUERKRAUT AT AN
APPROXIMATE VELOCITY OF 78.6 M.P.H

EVERY FACET OF THE OPERATION
WAS PLANNED WITH METICULOUS
ATTENTION TO DETAIL

HEINRICH COULD ALWAYS BE RELIED
UPON TO SERVE COFFEE IN HIS OWN
INIMITABLE STYLE

WE HAD NOT QUITE REALIZED THE FULL
EXTENT OF NORMAN'S CHICKPEA PROBLEM

UNDER THE NEW DIRECTIVES FROM BRUSSELS,
MRS HAMILTON WAS ABLE TO REPLENISH
THE CUSTARD EVERY OTHER THURSDAY

HIS CRÊPES WERE KNOWN AND
FEARED THROUGHOUT ORPINGTON

AS DARKNESS FELL, HE SOUGHT
TO IMPRESS ME WITH HIS RIGATONI

THE LADS KNEW PRECISELY WHAT TO DO
WITH KEVIN'S AUBERGINE FLAPJACKS

IT SEEMED POSSIBLE THAT THEY
MIGHT AT ONE TIME HAVE BEEN SPROUTS

THE TWINS WERE NOT NOTED FOR
THEIR LOVE OF FRESH VEGETABLES

ROBIN'S DESPERATE ATTEMPTS TO KICK-START THE SHERWOOD
ECONOMY WERE VIEWED WITH MORE THAN A DEGREE OF
SKEPTICISM BY THE LITIGATION DEPARTMENT

"TO MY MIND THERE'S NO FINER SIGHT
THAN KALE MOVING AT SPEED"
OPINED MILLWARD

"I HAVE A NASTY FEELING IT MAY WELL BE MOUSSAKA" STAMMERED BEN

WITH A SUDDEN FLOURISH HE
PRODUCED THE WHELK AND SO
ENDED THIRTEEN MONTHS OF
TENSION, UNEASE AND SPECULATION

TOGETHER WE WERE ABLE TO REMOVE
ALL TRACES OF THE INCRIMINATING TOFU

FOLLOWING UNCLE FRANK'S DIRECTIONS TO
THE NEAREST ITALIAN BAKERY REQUIRED
STAMINA AND AN UNSHAKABLE FAITH IN
HIS MASTERY OF LOCAL GEOGRAPHY

THE INCRIMINATING BAGUETTES WERE PLACED
UNDER ROUND THE CLOCK SURVEILLANCE

THE PREPARATION OF BRENDA'S
PACKED LUNCH WAS USUALLY
COMPLETED JUST BEFORE DAWN

IT WAS A BRAZEN ATTEMPT BY
MRS GRUNDEL TO LURE US INSIDE AGAIN

HOURS OF SILENCE FOLLOWED, PUNCTUATED
ONLY BY THE ALMOST IMPERCEPTIBLE SOUND
OF THE HAWSER LEAVING AND ENTERING
THE SAGO.......

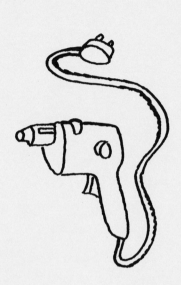

Number 1   *The Orange*

Number 2   The Grape

Number 3   The Banana

Number 4   The Strawberry

Number 5   The Pear

Number 6   The Greengage

Number 7 The Cranberry

Number 8   The Fig

Number 9   The Durian

Number 10   *The Apricot*

Number 11   The Lychee

Number 12   *The Kumquat*

Seared Luncheon Meat Ghentoise

Ingredients: 1 tin luncheon meat
2 fl oz balsamic vinegar
10oz sago
1 tablespoon extra virgin olive oil
mint leaf

Cooking Method: Empty contents of tin onto wooden board.
Slice carefully into 118 pieces. Set aside.
Prepare sago as per instructions on packet.
Heat a sturdy griddle. Wipe slices of
luncheon meat with oil. Toss and sear on
griddle. Add vinegar to sago and place on a
warmed chafing dish. Scatter luncheon
meat over sago and decorate with mint leaf.
(Serves 6)

Pädsköttel (Horse Droppings)

Trokene alte Brötchen in Wasser einweichen und zerkneten.
Mit einer feingehackten Zwiebel, etwas Petersilie zwei Eiern,
Salz, Pfeffer und Senf unter 500 g Gehacktes mischen. Die
Masse gut durchkneten und daraus kleine oder grosse
Bällchen formen. Ab damit in die heisse Pfanne. Schmecken
heiss und Kalt, aber vor allem mit scharfem Senf.

A Bavarian delicacy

New Ways
With
Vegetables
1

Aubergines

New Ways
With
Vegetables
2

Parsnips

New Ways
With
Vegetables
3

Garden Peas

New Ways
With
Vegetables

4

String Beans

"I'VE ASSIGNED TWO MEN TO REMOVE THE
OFFENDING FALAFEL" REASSURED SVEN

UNFORTUNATELY HIS THREAT OF A SARDINE
FONDUE HAD BECOME A GRIM REALITY

IT WAS NOT TOO LONG BEFORE
MRS TRINDLE'S OMELETTES BECAME
THE TALK OF THE HUNTER VALLEY

SOMEHOW IT SEEMED CHURLISH TO
BE CRITICAL OF A MAN WHO HAD SUCH
A WINNING WAY WITH RADICCHIO

DAPHNE HAD A TELLING WAY
WITH MACKEREL

GERALD FELT HE WAS QUITE CLOSE TO
SOLVING THE PROBLEM OF CATERING
FOR THE NEW PETS

THE ARRIVAL OF THE VEGETARIAN
SAUSAGE ROLL WAS ALWAYS THE
HIGHLIGHT OF THE FAMILY PICNIC

RICHARD HAD DEVISED AN INNOVATIVE
LOW-CALORIE SALAD DRESSING

I BEGAN TO NURTURE A SUSPICION THAT I
MIGHT POSSIBLY BE IN THE PRESENCE OF
THOSE WHO WERE NOT STRICT VEGETARIANS

GREAT
MOMENTS
IN HISTORY
Number 41

THE BIRTH OF IN-FLIGHT CATERING
Lunch, May 16ᵗ 1912   Altitude 1,232 feet

FROM TIME TO TIME I HAD TO ISSUE
A GENTLE REMINDER TO TIM TO ENSURE
MY EGGS WERE COOKED "OVER EASY"

EDWIN WAS QUICK TO DEMONSTRATE
HIS TECHNIQUE FOR COOKING SUSHI

RICHARD'S IDEA OF THE PERFECT PICNIC
DID NOT QUITE CORRESPOND TO THE
NOTION HELD SO DEAR BY SUSAN

ONLY THE DISTANT THUD OF QUICHE
UPON CONCRETE SUGGESTED TO FRANK
THAT SPRING WAS ALMOST HERE

I WAS DETERMINED TO ENSURE THAT
UNCLE FRANK'S BIRTHDAY CAKE WOULD
NOT BE FORGOTTEN IN A HURRY

AS A WAY OF FILLING BROGUES
WITH GUACAMOLE, IT WAS CLEARLY
IN A CLASS OF ITS OWN

JANET'S LEEK AND LOBSTER TERRINE SET
BOLD NEW STANDARDS IN THE ART
OF CULINARY PRESENTATION

ANNA SLIPPED QUIETLY AWAY LEAVING
HER GUESTS TO SAVOUR THE BROCCOLI
CROQUETTES IN A BALSAMIC DRESSING

UNFORTUNATELY PIERRE HAD A
LONG HISTORY OF *STILTON ABUSE*

THE SUDDEN APPEARANCE OF A LIMP, TRANSLUCENT
SPROUT COULD ONLY HERALD THE ONSLAUGHT
OF THE ANNUAL CHRISTMAS ORDEAL

Mexican Tofu

1. Take one sombrero
2. Invert
3. Fill with tofu
4. Allow to stand for 38 minutes

serves 80

Paupiettes de Pilchards Royale

Ingredients:

1 tin pilchards
2 oz butter (unsalted)
2 oz onions
2 oz breadcrumbs
4 oz minced carrots
1 tablespoon chopped parsley
1 oz flour
2 oz double cream. Pinch of nutmeg

Cooking Method:

Place all ingredients in mixing bowl.
Empty pilchards into mixture, beating
until thoroughly amalgamated. Mould
into ten spheres. Poach spheres in a
saucepan of cider for twenty minutes.
Drain and serve on a bed of roast lettuce
and shredded gherkin.

Serving Suggestions

Number 236: Brussels Sprouts

10 Interesting New Ways to serve Tofu

Serving Suggestions

Number 234
   A Rietveld Egg and
      Anchovy Salad

Serving Suggestions

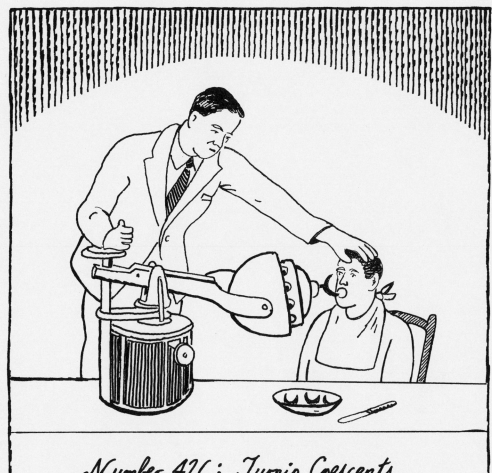

Number 426 : Turnip Crescents

Serving Suggestions

Number 63: Sweet Corn Medley

Serving Suggestions

Number 286: Warm Salad of Tuna with Salsa Verde

Serving Suggestions

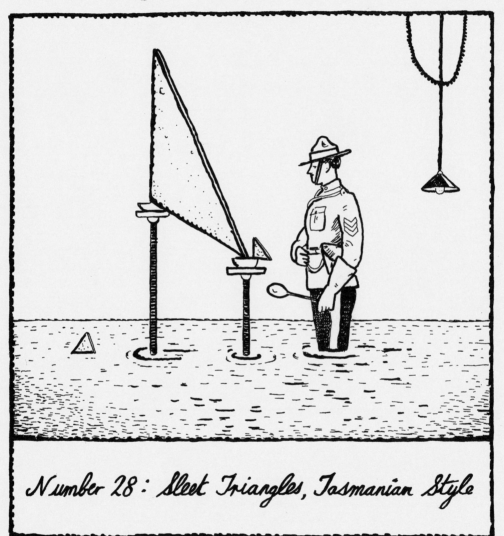

Number 28: Sleet Triangles, Tasmanian Style

Serving Suggestions

Number 226: Moussaka

"IT'S MY VERSION OF SUMMER PUDDING"
ANNOUNCED JAN PROUDLY

SHARING MY SANDWICH WITH ERIC
MARKED THE BEGINNING OF A LONG,
SERIOUSLY TROUBLED WEEKEND

"I FEEL THAT A DASH OF KETCHUP DOES
SO ENHANCE A MEAL" NOTED ROBERT

THE MAIN COURSE APPEARED TO HAVE
BEEN SLIGHTLY OVERSALTED

"THIS IS HOW I LIKE MY EGGS PREPARED!" ROARED THE STOKER

"I THINK YOU'LL FIND THAT IS YOUR MAIN COURSE, SIR" CORRECTED THE STYLIST

"I HAVE SOME RATHER
UNPLEASANT NEWS
FOR YOU, MRS CRYMM
— ONE OF THE TWO
PEOPLE IN THIS ROOM
IS A CANNIBAL...."

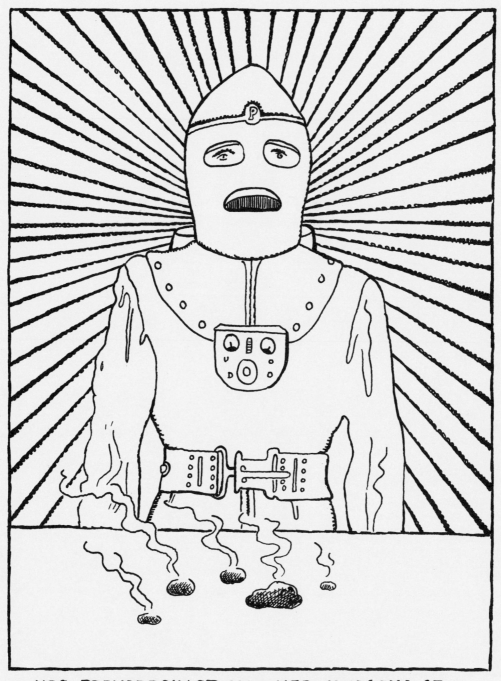

MRS PRENDERGHAST HAD HER OWN WAY OF
TURNING EVERY MEAL INTO A SPECIAL OCCASION

THE ARRIVAL OF TARAMASALATA
WAS GREETED WITH LESS THAN
UNANIMOUS APPROVAL

DURING HIS YEARS OUT EAST EVANS
HAD LEARNED TO APPROACH AN OVER-
RIPE BRIE WITH AN ELEMENT OF CAUTION

OUR LITTLE PICNIC SEEMED TO BE
PROGRESSING QUITE SMOOTHLY

HE WAS A FIRM BELIEVER
IN CONVENIENCE FOODS

AUNT AMELIA'S HOMEMADE LENTIL
SOUP WAS GOING DOWN A TREAT

"ARE YOU ABSOLUTELY CERTAIN THIS IS MY VEGETARIAN PLATTER, ENID?" QUERIED JANET

THE APPEARANCE OF THE WORDS "PRAWN
COCKTAIL" ON THE MENU WAS A CAUSE
FOR GENUINE CONCERN

"INCIDENTALLY, WAS THERE ANY FOOD INVOLVED IN THE PREPARATION OF THIS MEAL?" QUERIED THE CONNOISSEUR

ASKING SIMON TO LEND A HAND
IN THE KITCHEN WAS ALWAYS
A BIG MISTAKE...

IT SEEMED THAT THE BRAISED CABBAGE
MET WITH NIGEL'S TACIT APPROVAL

IT SEEMED CLARISSA HAD LOCATED
THE MISSING BRATWURST

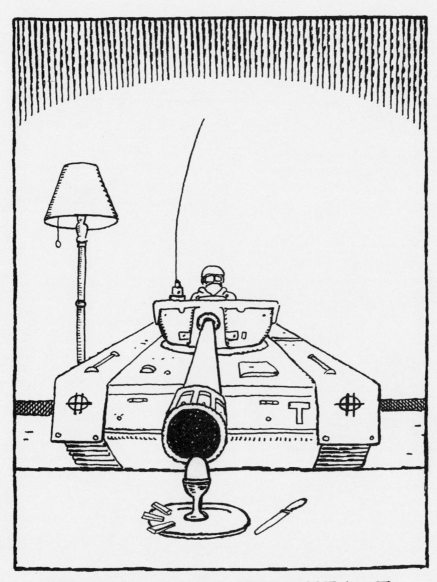

BRENDA TOOK BREAKFAST
VERY SERIOUSLY

THE ARRIVAL OF FRESH STRAWBERRIES
DID LITTLE TO LIGHTEN MRS SNORNBY'S
SOMBRE MOOD

THE CAESAR SALAD CAME
HIGHLY RECOMMENDED

"FEELING PECKISH AGAIN, DEAR?" MURMURED MIRIAM

"I PREFER TO USE MY OWN CUTLERY,
THANKS" HISSED GREG PETULANTLY

THOSE SPECIAL OCCASIONS

"IT'S YOUR FAVOURITE SORBET, DEAR"
EXPLAINED MIRANDA

OUR SELF-CATERING HOLIDAY WAS
TURNING OUT TO BE A BIG SUCCESS

IT WAS MY FIRST VISIT
TO A DUTCH RESTAURANT

IT BECAME APPARENT THAT BRENDA
WOULD NOT BE SHARING HER MEATBALL
WITH THE REST OF US AFTER ALL

SOMETIMES EDWIN WOULD THREATEN
US WITH AN OMELETTE

IT WAS MY JOB TO REMOVE ANY
MORSELS OF LEFT-OVER FOOD FROM
MRS DROINBIRTLE'S TABLE

BY SUBSTITUTING LINOLEUM FOR MAIZE
FLOUR, MAX APPEARED TO HAVE MADE
A SIGNIFICANT BREAKTHROUGH IN
THE PRODUCTION OF HIS TORTILLAS

"I TAKE IT THE STUFFED SUNFLOWER
SEEDS IN TURNIP MAYONNAISE ARE FOR
YOU, MADAM?" SNAPPED THE MARTINET

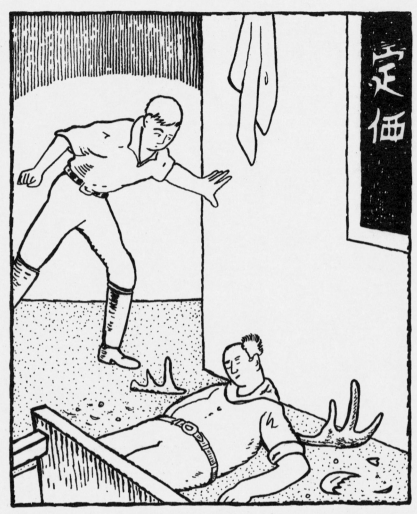

I WAS TOO LATE. HE HAD ALREADY
ORDERED THE ROAST ELK AND CHILLI
SALAD ON A BED OF WITHERED LEEKS

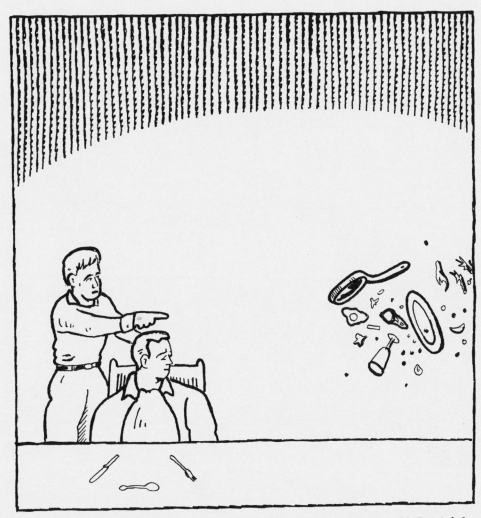

"LUNCH HERE TENDS TO BE AN INFORMAL
AFFAIR" EXPLAINED ROGER

A selection of Glen Baxter's
tableware is available from
Poole Pottery, The Quay, Poole
Dorset BH15 1RE